Delicious Desserts

From Light to Luscious

THE
AMERICAN
·COOKING·
GUILD

Acknowledgments:
—Recipes developed by the Current® Test Kitchen
—Cover photo by Burwell & Burwell
—Illustrations by Jim Haynes
—Design & typesetting by BOSS Services

ISBN 0–942320–51–4

More Great Cookbooks!
Send $1.00 for a color catalog of our cookbooks. Your $1.00 will be applied to your first order.

Published by:
The American Cooking Guild
6–A East Cedar Avenue
Gaithersburg, MD 20877
301-963-0698

Contents

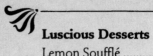

Luscious Desserts

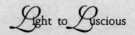

Introduction

Who doesn't enjoy a nice dessert? Somehow, a special treat at the end of a meal makes us feel happy and satisfied. It's often the most enjoyable part of the meal as we linger at the table to talk over a cup of steaming coffee and a slice of cake or a creamy ice cream confection.

In planning this book, we wanted to accommodate everyone who enjoys desserts, regardless of the calories involved. We've included both recipes considered light and healthy, and ones that are rich and luscious.

When you're trying to watch calories and fat, it doesn't mean an end to desserts—just a new approach to what some consider to be an essential part of the meal. The light desserts in this book have about 200 calories or less per serving. Even a weight-watcher can indulge—just keep track of your total calorie intake each day. We've done our best to make these low-calorie desserts really tasty.

Sometimes we want to indulge in something extra special, and to heck with the calories. Perhaps company is coming, it's a family member's birthday or there is another special occasion to celebrate. Let's enjoy a rich dessert tonight, and we can always go for an extra long walk or cut back on calories tomorrow to make up for the extravagance. The calories for luscious desserts have no limits, but they are well worth it in terms of enjoyment.

At the end of each recipe, we list the calories per serving, along with other nutrient values for those of you on special diets or just interested in knowing the nutritional content of your daily meals. We're sure you'll find irresistible recipes in both sections of this book to please your family and friends.

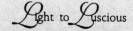

Light Desserts

Cold Raspberry Soufflé

Elegant but easy to fix.

- 2 packages (10 oz. each) frozen red raspberries in heavy syrup, thawed
- 2 envelopes unflavored gelatin
- 1/2 cup cold water
- 3 large egg whites, at room temperature
- 2 tablespoons sugar
- 1 1/4 cups whipping cream, whipped

Place raspberries with syrup in a blender container. Cover and blend until puréed. Over a large bowl, press purée through a sieve with a rubber scraper to remove seeds.

In a small saucepan, mix gelatin and water; let stand for 1 minute. Stir over low heat until gelatin dissolves. Stir into raspberry purée; set aside.

In a large mixer bowl at high speed, beat egg whites until soft peaks form. Gradually beat in sugar and continue beating until stiff and glossy; set aside.

Place bowl of purée in a larger bowl that contains cold water and ice. Stir raspberry mixture until it begins to thicken. Remove bowl from ice water.

Fold in beaten egg whites and 2 cups of the whipped cream. Pour into a serving dish. Refrigerate at least 1 hour or until set.

Top with dollops of remaining whipped cream. Garnish with lime slices if desired.

Makes 10 (about 1/2 cup) servings

Per serving:

- 181 calories
- 3.2 gm. protein
- 11.1 gm. fat
- 18.3 gm. carbohydrate
- 28.9 mg. sodium
- 42.0 mg. cholesterol
- 29.8 mg. calcium

Citrus Chiffon

This can also be used as a filling for tart shells.

3/4	cup sugar
1	envelope unflavored gelatin
3	medium oranges
1	tablespoon lemon juice
2	large egg yolks
4	large egg whites, at room temperature

In a small saucepan, mix 1/2 cup of the sugar and gelatin; set aside.

Grate orange rind to make 1 teaspoon; set aside. Squeeze oranges to make 1 cup juice. Stir orange and lemon juices into gelatin; let stand for 1 minute. Stir over low heat until gelatin dissolves. Remove from heat.

In a small bowl, beat egg yolks well. Gradually stir about one-third of the hot mixture into egg yolks, then stir back into hot mixture in saucepan. Cook and stir over low heat until slightly thickened (do not boil). Remove from heat. Stir in reserved orange rind.

Place saucepan in a large bowl that contains cold water and ice. Stir gelatin mixture until it mounds when dropped from a spoon, about 5 minutes. Remove saucepan from ice water; set aside.

In a small mixer bowl at high speed, beat egg whites until soft peaks form. Gradually beat in remaining 1/4 cup sugar and beat until stiff peaks form. Stir about 1/2 cup of the whites into gelatin mixture. Fold in remaining whites until no white streaks remain. Spoon into six dessert dishes. Chill at least 1 hour.

Makes 6 (about 2/3 cup) servings

Per serving:

151	calories
4.5	gm. protein
1.9	gm. fat
29.7	gm. carbohydrate
37.9	mg. sodium
90.7	mg. cholesterol
16.5	mg. calcium

Light

Victorian Cherry Blossoms

Almond and cherry are delicious together.

1	envelope unflavored gelatin
2	cups skim milk
1/4	cup sugar
1/2	teaspoon almond extract
1/2	teaspoon vanilla extract
6	tablespoons cherry preserves

In a 1-quart saucepan, mix gelatin and 1 cup of the skim milk; let stand for 1 minute. Add sugar. Stir over low heat until gelatin dissolves.

Stir in remaining 1 cup skim milk, almond extract and vanilla. Pour into four 6-ounce custard cups or dessert dishes or 1/2-cup molds. Cover and chill at least 2 hours or until set.

To serve, unmold onto individual dessert plates if desired. Top each with 1 1/2 tablespoons of the preserves.

Makes 4 (1/2 cup) servings

Per serving:

182	calories
5.8	gm. protein
0.2	gm. fat
39.6	gm. carbohydrate
68.1	mg. sodium
2.0	mg. cholesterol
157.0	mg. calcium

Strawberries in Ginger Cream

The ginger adds a unique flavor.

2	cups strawberries
3/4	cup dairy sour cream
3	tablespoons brown sugar
1 1/2	tablespoons finely chopped crystallized ginger

Slice strawberries and place in a medium bowl; set aside.

In a small bowl, stir sour cream, brown sugar and crystallized ginger until blended.

Just before serving, stir sour cream mixture into strawberries until blended. Spoon into small dessert dishes. Garnish with mint leaves if desired.

Makes 4 (about 2/3 cup) servings

Per serving:

151	calories
1.6	gm. protein
7.8	gm. fat
19.7	gm. carbohydrate
22.1	mg. sodium
15.0	mg. cholesterol
61.3	mg. calcium

Light

Papayas Tropicale

Ripen papayas at room temperature for maximum sweetness.

1	*medium ripe banana*
1/2	*cup strawberries*
1	*drop red food color*
2	*papayas*
2	*cups small honeydew melon balls, drained*
2	*whole strawberries or 4 mint leaves*

Cut banana in pieces and slice strawberries. Place in a blender container and add food color. Cover and blend until smooth. Sauce can be used immediately or covered and refrigerated up to 1 hour.

Just before serving, cut each papaya in half lengthwise; remove seeds. Place each papaya half on a dessert plate. Spoon sauce into papayas. Top with honeydew. Garnish with strawberries or mint leaves.

Makes 4 servings

Per serving:

121	calories
1.7	gm. protein
0.5	gm. fat
30.7	gm. carbohydrate
13.0	mg. sodium
0.0	mg. cholesterol
45.6	mg. calcium

Fall Fruit Compote

A good dessert for a buffet meal.

1	*can (20 oz.) pineapple chunks in juice*
1	*medium orange*
1	*medium pear*
6	*maraschino cherries, halved*
1	*tablespoon cornstarch*
1/4	*teaspoon ground ginger*

Drain pineapple juice into a 1-cup measuring cup. Add enough water to make 1 cup liquid; set liquid aside. Peel and section orange. Cut each section in half. Peel and slice pear, removing center core.

Place pineapple, orange, pear and cherries in a medium bowl or plastic container; set fruit aside.

In a small saucepan, stir together cornstarch and ginger. Slowly stir in reserved pineapple liquid until smooth. Stirring constantly over medium heat, bring to a boil and boil for 1 minute or until thick and shiny.

Pour hot sauce over fruit; toss gently to coat. Cover and chill at least 1 hour.

Serve in small dessert dishes.

Makes 6 (2/3 cup) servings

Per serving:

98	calories
0.7	gm. protein
0.2	gm. fat
25.1	gm. carbohydrate
1.7	mg. sodium
0.0	mg. cholesterol
24.8	mg. calcium

Deluxe Strawberry Dessert Cups

Neufchatel is a low-calorie cream cheese.

3	cups strawberries
2	tablespoons sugar
3	ounces Neufchatel cream cheese, softened
1/2	cup vanilla lowfat yogurt
1/2	teaspoon vanilla extract
6	sponge shortcake dessert cups (1 oz. each)

Slice strawberries and place 1 cup of the slices in a blender container. Cover and blend until puréed.

In a medium bowl, stir remaining strawberries, strawberry purée and sugar. Let stand at room temperature for 20 minutes.

In a small bowl, beat or whisk cream cheese until smooth and fluffy. Stir in yogurt and vanilla until blended.

To assemble, spoon equal amounts of strawberries and juice into shortcake cups. Spoon sauce over. Serve or let stand up to 1 hour to let juice soak into cake.

Makes 6 servings

Per serving:

166	calories
4.7	gm. protein
5.3	gm. fat
25.9	gm. carbohydrate
111.9	mg. sodium
11.9	mg. cholesterol
61.0	mg. calcium

Cherry Freeze

If using fresh sweet cherries, pit, then freeze before processing.

1   package (16 oz.) frozen pitted dark sweet cherries (about 4 cups)
4   tablespoons powdered sugar
2/3   cup half-and-half
1/2   teaspoon almond extract
1/2   teaspoon vanilla extract

Place cherries in a food processor bowl. Cover and process with on-off bursts until finely chopped. With motor running, add powdered sugar through feed tube, 1 tablespoon at a time. Then add half-and-half, almond extract and vanilla and process until well blended and creamy, scraping sides of bowl as needed.

Pour into a freezer container. Place a piece of plastic wrap directly on surface and freeze for 1 to 11/2 hours or until mixture is the consistency of ice cream.

Stir before serving.

Makes 6 (about 1/2 cup) servings

Per serving:

111   calories
1.7   gm. protein
3.7   gm. fat
18.8   gm. carbohydrate
11.1   mg. sodium
10.6   mg. cholesterol
39.1   mg. calcium

Frozen Pumpkin Dessert

If desired, garnish with whipped topping and sprinkle with pumpkin pie spice.

10	*gingersnaps*
2	*teaspoons margarine, melted*
1	*cup canned pumpkin*
1/2	*cup sugar*
1 1/4	*teaspoons pumpkin pie spice*
1	*quart vanilla lowfat frozen yogurt, softened*

Lightly coat a 1 1/2-quart oblong baking dish with nonstick cooking spray.

Place gingersnaps in a blender container. Cover and blend until finely crushed (you will need about 1/2 cup). Transfer to a small bowl. Add margarine and stir until crumbs are evenly coated. Evenly pat into bottom of dish.

In a medium bowl, stir pumpkin, sugar and pumpkin pie spice until well blended.

In a large bowl, stir frozen yogurt until smooth but not melted. Stir in pumpkin mixture just until well blended. Carefully pour into baking dish. Place plastic wrap directly on surface. Cover dish with foil. Freeze for 4 hours or until firm. Can be made up to 1 week before serving.

To serve, cut with a sharp knife.

Makes 8 servings

Per serving:

197	calories
3.9	gm. protein
3.4	gm. fat
38.7	gm. carbohydrate
130.8	mg. sodium
10	mg. cholesterol
117.1	mg. calcium

Kiwifruit Sorbetti

Use fully ripe fruit for the best flavor.

1	cup water
1/2	cup sugar
1/2	cup light corn syrup
3	kiwifruit
1/4	teaspoon grated lemon rind
5	teaspoons lemon juice

In a small saucepan, mix water, sugar and corn syrup. Stirring over high heat, cook until sugar dissolves. Remove from heat.

Peel and slice kiwifruit and place in a food processor bowl or blender container. Cover and process or blend until puréed (you will need 3/4 cup). Stir into sugar mixture. Add lemon rind and juice. Pour into an 8 x 8 x 2-inch baking pan. Cover and freeze for 1 hour or until firm but not hard.

Break into pieces. Transfer to a chilled small mixer bowl. With chilled beaters, beat at low speed until smooth and fluffy but not melted. Serve immediately or cover and freeze up to 2 hours or until firm enough to scoop but not hard.

Makes 5 (about 1/2 cup) servings

Per serving:

200	calories
0.5	gm. protein
0.2	gm. fat
51.8	gm. carbohydrate
25.0	mg. sodium
0.0	mg. cholesterol
26.9	mg. calcium

Chocolate Almond Cups

Rich and creamy. No one would guess these are low in calories.

1/3	cup slivered almonds
1	large egg white, at room temperature
1/8	teaspoon salt
2	tablespoons sugar
1	envelope whipped topping mix (will make 2 cups)
	Cold skim milk (about 1/2 cup)
1	teaspoon vanilla extract
1/4	teaspoon almond extract
2	tablespoons unsweetened cocoa powder
1/2	teaspoon chocolate decors

Preheat oven to 350°. In a shallow pan, bake almonds for 5 to 8 minutes or until toasted, stirring occasionally for even browning. Set aside to cool. Place in a food processor bowl or blender container. Cover and process or blend until ground; set aside.

In a small mixer bowl at high speed, beat egg white and salt until soft peaks form. Gradually beat in sugar until glossy and stiff peaks form. Transfer to a large bowl.

Prepare topping according to package directions, substituting skim milk for whole milk, using 1 teaspoon vanilla and adding almond extract. Stir half of the whipped topping into egg white. Fold in remaining whipped topping, ground almonds and cocoa powder until no white streaks remain. Spoon into six paper cup-lined muffin pan cups or small dessert dishes. Sprinkle with chocolate decors. Freeze at least 6 hours or overnight.

Can be eaten straight from the freezer.

Makes 6 (about 1/2 cup) servings

Per serving:

119	calories
3.3	gm. protein
6.8	gm. fat
10.9	gm. carbohydrate
70.4	mg. sodium
0.3	mg. cholesterol
49.6	mg. calcium

Mocha Bavarian

A good substitute for chocolate mousse.

1	envelope unflavored gelatin
1 1/2	cups cold skim milk
1/3	cup sugar
2	tablespoons unsweetened cocoa powder
1	tablespoon instant coffee granules
1	teaspoon vanilla extract
1/2	cup frozen nondairy whipped topping, thawed
1	large egg white, at room temperature
6	tablespoons frozen nondairy whipped topping, thawed

In a small saucepan, mix gelatin and skim milk; let stand for 1 minute. Whisk in sugar, cocoa powder and coffee granules. Stir over low heat until gelatin dissolves.

Pour gelatin mixture into a large metal bowl. Stir in vanilla. Place bowl in a larger bowl of cold water and ice. Stir gelatin mixture until it is the consistency of unbeaten egg whites. Remove bowl from ice water. Stir in 1/2 cup whipped topping.

In a small mixer bowl at high speed, beat egg white until soft peaks form. Fold into gelatin mixture until no white streaks remain. Pour into six 4-ounce stemmed dessert glasses or dessert dishes. Chill for 1 hour or until set.

Garnish each serving with 1 tablespoon of the whipped topping.

Makes 6 (about 1/2 cup) servings

Per serving:

114	calories
4.1	gm. protein
2.7	gm. fat
17.7	gm. carbohydrate
44.5	mg. sodium
1.0	mg. cholesterol
80.3	mg. calcium

Meringue Shells

Makes impressive crisp shells for any filling.

4	*large egg whites, at room temperature*
1/8	*teaspoon cream of tartar*
1	*cup sugar*

Preheat oven to 225°. Line a baking sheet with brown paper.

In a small mixer bowl at high speed, beat egg whites until foamy. Add cream of tartar and beat until soft peaks form. Gradually beat in sugar and continue beating until stiff peaks form and sugar dissolves. Spoon onto brown paper, making eight mounds 3 inches apart. Shape each into a 3-inch circle with an indentation in the center.

Bake for 1 hour. Turn oven off and with oven door closed, cool for 1 hour. Cool meringues completely on a wire rack; remove from brown paper. Store in an airtight container.

To serve, fill each shell with about 1/3 cup of Cream Filling (see page 20). Or fill with lowfat frozen yogurt or fresh fruit.

Makes 8 shells

Per shell:

104	calories
1.7	gm. protein
0.0	gm. fat
25.1	gm. carbohydrate
25.2	mg. sodium
0.0	mg. cholesterol
2.0	mg. calcium

Cream Filling

This can be used to fill the Meringue Shells on page 19, or it can be spooned into dishes and garnished with fruit.

1¹/2   *cups skim milk*
1   *package (3¹/2 oz.) vanilla instant pudding and pie filling mix*
1   *envelope whipped topping mix (will make 2 cups)*
¹/2   *teaspoon vanilla or rum extract*
    Meringue Shells (see page 19)

Chill a small mixer bowl and beaters.

In chilled mixer bowl at low speed, beat skim milk, pudding and pie filling mix, whipped topping mix and vanilla or rum extract until blended. Increase speed to high and beat for 4 minutes or until thick and fluffy, scraping sides of bowl occasionally.

Pipe or spoon into meringue shells. Chill at least 1 hour or up to 4 hours.

Makes 8 (about ¹/3 cup) servings

Per serving:

89   calories
1.9   gm. protein
2.2   gm. fat
16.0   gm. carbohydrate
83.7   mg. sodium
0.7   mg. cholesterol
56.8   mg. calcium

Maple Caramel Custard

When unmolded, the custard has its own maple-flavored sauce on top.

1	cup sugar
4	large eggs
1³/4	cups skim milk
1/2	teaspoon vanilla extract
1/2	teaspoon liquid maple flavor

Preheat oven to 350°.

Place 1/2 cup of the sugar in a small, heavy saucepan. Stirring constantly over low heat, melt sugar until it turns into a golden brown syrup. Quickly pour evenly into bottoms of six 6-ounce custard cups; set aside.

In a medium bowl, whisk eggs. Add skim milk, remaining sugar, vanilla and maple flavor and whisk until well blended. Pour about 1/2 cup of the mixture into each custard cup. Place cups in a 12 x 9 x 2-inch baking pan. Place in oven; fill pan with boiling water to a depth of 1 inch.

Bake for 40 to 50 minutes or until a knife inserted near center of custards comes out clean. Remove cups from water bath. Cool custards on a wire rack for 15 minutes, then chill at least 2 hours.

To serve, carefully run a small metal spatula or tip of a knife around edge of custards to release from cups. Unmold onto individual dessert plates.

Makes 6 (1/2 cup) servings

Per serving:

207	calories
6.5	gm. protein
3.8	gm. fat
37.2	gm. carbohydrate
83.1	mg. sodium
183.8	mg. cholesterol
106.7	mg. calcium

Orange Rice Custard

The pan of boiling water keeps the custard from curdling.

1²/3   cups skim milk
3   large eggs
1/2   cup sugar
1/3   cup raw instant rice
1   teaspoon vanilla extract
1   teaspoon orange extract
1/2   teaspoon grated orange rind
   Dash of salt
   Ground nutmeg

Preheat oven to 350°.

Coat a 1-quart deep casserole with nonstick cooking spray.

In a small saucepan over medium heat, heat skim milk until very hot (do not boil).

Meanwhile, in a medium bowl, beat eggs. Stir in sugar, rice, vanilla, orange extract, orange rind and salt.

Stir in hot milk. Pour into casserole. Place casserole in a 9 x 9 x 2-inch or larger baking pan. Place in oven; fill pan with boiling water to a depth of 1 inch.

Bake for 10 minutes. Stir. Bake for 10 minutes. Stir. Sprinkle with nutmeg and bake 10 to 15 minutes longer or until a knife inserted 1 inch from center comes out clean. Remove casserole from water bath. Cool custard on a wire rack.

Serve at room temperature or chill at least 1 hour and serve cold.

Makes 5 (1/2 cup) servings

Per serving:

181   calories
6.9   gm. protein
3.5   gm. fat
30.1   gm. carbohydrate
134.8   mg. sodium
165.7   mg. cholesterol
118.5   mg. calcium

Pineapple and Rum Dessert

To use fresh pineapple, cut rings about one-half inch thick.

 4 *canned pineapple rings in juice, drained and juice reserved*
 1/4 *teaspoon rum extract*
 2 *tablespoons brown sugar*
  Ground cinnamon
 4 *whole strawberries*

Place top oven shelf about 6 inches from heat source. Preheat oven to 375°.

Place pineapple rings in a 9 x 9 x 2-inch baking dish or 9-inch pie plate; sprinkle with 2 tablespoons of the pineapple juice and rum extract. Save remaining pineapple juice for another use. Let stand for 10 minutes, basting pineapple occasionally.

Bake on top shelf of oven for 10 minutes. Baste each pineapple slice with juice and sprinkle with 1 1/2 teaspoons of the brown sugar. Turn oven temperature to broil. Broil for 1 to 2 minutes or until sugar is caramelized. Baste with juice and sprinkle with cinnamon (about 1/8 teaspoon total).

Serve pineapple immediately on small dessert plates. Top each with a strawberry.

Makes 4 servings

Per serving:

  70 calories
  0.3 gm. protein
  0.1 gm. fat
 18.2 gm. carbohydrate
  3.2 mg. sodium
  0.0 mg. cholesterol
 17.8 mg. calcium

Mandarin Crepes

3/4	cup skim milk
2	large eggs
6	tablespoons cornstarch
1	tablespoon vegetable oil
2	teaspoons sugar
3/4	teaspoon baking powder
1/4	teaspoon salt
1/3	cup sugar
1/3	cup orange juice
2	tablespoons margarine
1	can (11 oz.) mandarin orange segments, well drained

Place skim milk, eggs, cornstarch, oil, 2 teaspoons sugar, baking powder and salt in a blender container. Cover and blend.

Heat a heavy nonstick 6-inch skillet over medium-high heat. Coat skillet lightly with nonstick cooking spray. Pour about 2 tablespoons of the batter into skillet and quickly tilt skillet to spread evenly across bottom and 1/2 inch up sides. Cook for 30 seconds to 1 minute or until bottom is lightly browned; turn crepe. Cook briefly. Invert onto a plate. Continue until all batter is used.

In a small saucepan over medium-low heat, cook and stir 1/3 cup sugar, orange juice and margarine until margarine melts. Without stirring, simmer for 5 minutes or until slightly thickened. Remove from heat. Cover and keep warm. To assemble, roll crepes individually and place two on each dessert plate. Place oranges on crepes and spoon 2 tablespoons warm sauce over each serving.

Makes 6 servings

Per serving:

186	calories
3.3	gm. protein
0.0	gm. fat
25.6	gm. carbohydrate
209.0	mg. sodium
91.8	mg. cholesterol
75.9	mg. calcium

Apple Sponge Pudding

Leftover pudding reheats well.

1/4	cup all-purpose flour
1/2	teaspoon baking powder
1/8	teaspoon salt
2	large eggs
1/2	cup sugar
1/2	teaspoon vanilla extract
2	medium Golden Delicious apples
1/4	cup raisins

Preheat oven to 325°. Lightly coat a 9-inch pie plate with nonstick cooking spray.

Into a small bowl, sift flour, baking powder and salt; set aside.

In a small mixer bowl at high speed, beat eggs, sugar and vanilla for 3 to 5 minutes or until fluffy and pale yellow. At low speed, beat in flour mixture until well blended.

Peel, core and coarsely chop apples (you will need 2 cups). Stir apples and raisins into batter. Pour into pie plate.

Bake for 30 minutes or until puffed in the center and golden brown on top.

Spoon into six dessert dishes. Serve warm.

Makes 6 servings

Per serving:

152	calories
2.8	gm. protein
2.1	gm. fat
31.6	gm. carbohydrate
87.5	mg. sodium
91.3	mg. cholesterol
32.1	mg. calcium

Baked Peaches and Blueberries

Fresh fruit can also be used, but baking time will vary.

1	bag (16 oz.) frozen unsweetened sliced peaches, thawed (4 cups)
2	cups frozen unsweetened blueberries, thawed
1/3	cup shredded coconut
1/4	cup sugar
1	tablespoon all-purpose flour
1/2	teaspoon ground cinnamon
1/4	teaspoon ground nutmeg

Preheat oven to 375°. Coat a 9 x 2-inch round baking dish with non-stick cooking spray.

Place peaches and blueberries in a large bowl; set aside.

In a small bowl, stir coconut, sugar, flour, cinnamon and nutmeg. Add to fruit and stir until fruit is coated. Spoon into baking dish.

Bake for 20 minutes. Stir. Cover dish loosely with foil. Bake 15 to 20 minutes longer or until very bubbly and peaches are tender. Uncover and cool slightly.

Stir before serving; serve warm.

Makes 8 (2/3 cup) servings

Per serving:

92	calories
0.9	gm. protein
1.6	gm. fat
20.3	gm. carbohydrate
12.4	mg. sodium
0.0	mg. cholesterol
8.1	mg. calcium

Light

Pineapple Cheesecake

No one would guess this is made with yogurt and cottage cheese.

1/2	cup sugar
1/4	cup all-purpose flour
2	large eggs
3/4	cup lowfat (2%) cottage cheese
1 1/2	teaspoons vanilla extract
3/4	teaspoon pineapple extract
5	drops yellow food color
1	container (8 oz.) plain lowfat yogurt
1/4	cup graham cracker crumbs (about 4 squares)
1	tablespoon margarine, melted

Preheat oven to 300°. Lightly coat a 7-inch deep-dish pie plate with nonstick cooking spray.

In a small bowl, mix sugar and flour; set aside.

Place eggs, cottage cheese, vanilla, pineapple extract and food color in a blender container. Cover and blend at low speed for 30 seconds or until smooth. With motor running at low speed, spoon in sugar-flour mixture, blending until smooth.

Add yogurt; blend just until combined. Pour into pie plate.

Bake for 30 minutes. In a small bowl, mix crumbs and margarine. Sprinkle over cheesecake. Bake 40 minutes longer or until center is puffed and set. Turn oven off. With oven door ajar, let cheesecake cool in oven for 30 minutes. Remove from oven and cool completely on a wire rack. Chill at least 1 hour.

Serve chilled.

Makes 6 servings

Per serving:

210	calories
9.0	gm. protein
5.7	gm. fat
30.6	gm. carbohydrate
242.4	mg. sodium
96.0	mg. cholesterol
102.7	mg. calcium

Piña Colada Yogurt Pie

3	tablespoons flaked coconut
7	(2¹/2-inch) crispy-style macaroon cookies
2	tablespoons margarine, melted
¹/3	cup sugar
1	envelope unflavored gelatin
1	cup cold water
2	large eggs, separated
1	container (8 oz.) piña colada lowfat yogurt
¹/8	teaspoon coconut extract
¹/8	teaspoon pineapple extract
2	tablespoons sugar

Preheat oven to 350°. Grease a 9-inch pie plate.

In a shallow pan, bake coconut for 5 minutes or until toasted.

Break up macaroon cookies. Place in a food processor or blender and process with on-off bursts to make fine crumbs (about 1 cup). In a small bowl, combine cookie crumbs and margarine. Press crumbs in bottom and halfway up sides of pie plate. Bake for 10 minutes. Cool on a wire rack.

In a small saucepan, stir together ¹/3 cup sugar and gelatin. Stir in water; let stand for 1 minute. Stir over low heat until gelatin dissolves.

Gradually stir gelatin mixture into beaten egg yolks, then stir back into saucepan. Cook and stir over low heat until slightly thickened (do not boil). Pour mixture into a medium bowl. Place bowl of gelatin mixture in a larger bowl of cold water and ice. Stir gelatin mixture until it mounds slightly when dropped from a spoon. Remove bowl from ice water. Stir in yogurt, coconut extract, and pineapple extract.

In a small mixer bowl at high speed, beat egg whites until soft peaks form. Gradually beat in 2 tablespoons sugar and continue beating until stiff peaks form. Fold into yogurt mixture until no white streaks remain. Spoon into cooled crust. Chill at least 2 hours. Garnish with coconut.

Makes 8 servings

Per serving:

215	calories	83.8	mg. sodium
4.4	gm. protein	69.7	mg. cholesterol
9.7	gm. fat	52.2	mg. calcium
28.9	gm. carbohydrate		

Light

Frozen Strawberry Roll

2	large eggs, separated
3	tablespoons sugar
1/2	teaspoon vanilla extract
1/2	cup all-purpose flour
1/2	teaspoon baking powder
1/8	teaspoon salt
1	tablespoon powdered sugar
1	cup strawberry lowfat frozen yogurt, softened
1 1/2	cups strawberries
2	teaspoons sugar
1/8	teaspoon vanilla extract

Preheat oven to 350°. Grease a 10 x 6 x 2-inch baking dish. Line inside of dish with waxed paper.

In a small mixer bowl at medium speed, beat egg yolks for 5 minutes or until thick. Gradually beat in 3 tablespoons sugar until sugar dissolves. Beat in 1/2 teaspoon vanilla. Wash beaters.

In a small mixer bowl at high speed, beat egg whites until soft peaks form. By hand, fold into egg yolks. Sift flour, baking powder and salt over the top. Fold in until flour mixture is moistened and no streaks remain. Spread in dish. Bake for 12 to 15 minutes or until top springs back when touched. Loosen edges and invert onto towel sprinkled with powdered sugar. Peel off waxed paper. Roll cake in towel starting at narrow end; place on a wire rack to cool completely.

Unroll cake and spread with frozen yogurt. Re-roll. Wrap in foil and freeze at least 4 hours. Place in refrigerator 30 minutes before serving.

Slice strawberries and place in a blender container. Add 2 teaspoons sugar and 1/8 teaspoon vanilla. Cover and blend until puréed.

To serve, slice cake roll and place slices on individual plates. Spoon purée over the top. Makes 4 servings

Per serving:

210	calories	174.6	mg. sodium
6.6	gm. protein	111.3	mg. cholesterol
3.6	gm. fat	109.4	mg. calcium
38.6	gm. carbohydrate		

Anna's Apricot Cake

1 1/4	cups all-purpose flour
1	teaspoon baking powder
1/4	teaspoon salt
1/3	cup sugar
3	tablespoons margarine, softened
1	large egg
1/4	cup water
1	teaspoon vanilla extract
1	can (16 oz.) apricot halves in extra light syrup, well drained
1/4	cup apricot preserves plus 1 tablespoon water
1	tablespoon sugar plus 1/4 teaspoon ground cinnamon
9	tablespoons frozen nondairy whipped topping, thawed

Preheat oven to 400°. Coat a 9 x 9 x 2-inch baking pan with nonstick cooking spray.

In a small bowl, stir together flour, baking powder and salt; set aside.

In a small mixer bowl at medium speed, beat 1/3 cup sugar and margarine until fluffy. Beat in egg. At low speed, beat in 1/4 cup water and vanilla. Add flour mixture. Beat for 2 minutes or until smooth, scraping sides of bowl occasionally. Spread evenly in pan (layer will be thin). Arrange apricot halves, rounded-side up, over batter.

In a small saucepan over low heat, bring preserves and 1 tablespoon water to a boil. Spoon evenly over apricots.

In a small bowl, stir together 1 tablespoon sugar and cinnamon. Sprinkle over preserves.

Bake for 25 minutes or until lightly browned and a wooden pick inserted in center of cake comes out clean. Cool on a wire rack. Serve warm with whipped topping.

Makes 9 servings

Per serving:

191	calories	142.4	mg. sodium
2.7	gm. protein	30.4	mg. cholesterol
5.6	gm. fat	35.0	mg. calcium
32.7	gm. carbohydrate		

Light

Sunshine Cake

1¹/3	cups all-purpose flour
1	cup sugar
1	teaspoon baking powder
¹/4	teaspoon salt
4	large eggs, separated
¹/4	cup vegetable oil
¹/4	cup water
1¹/2	teaspoons grated lemon rind
1	teaspoon vanilla extract
1	teaspoon lemon extract
3	drops yellow food color (optional)
¹/2	teaspoon cream of tartar
2	tablespoons powdered sugar

Preheat oven to 325°. Place oven rack in lower third of oven.

Into a small mixer bowl, sift flour, sugar, baking powder and salt. Add egg yolks, oil, water, lemon rind, vanilla, lemon extract and food color. At low speed, beat until flour is moistened. Beat at medium speed for 4 minutes or until thick and smooth, scraping bowl occasionally. Wash beaters.

In a large mixer bowl at high speed, beat egg whites and cream of tartar until stiff but not dry. By hand, stir about one-fourth of the egg whites into the yolk mixture. Then fold in remaining egg whites until no white streaks remain. Pour into an ungreased 10-inch tube pan.

Bake for 50 to 60 minutes or until top springs back when lightly touched with a finger. Invert pan on a rack and let cake cool completely before removing from pan. Just before serving, sprinkle with powered sugar. Cut with a serrated knife.

Makes 12 servings

Per serving:

184	calories	91.7	mg. sodium
3.4	gm. protein	90.7	mg. cholesterol
6.5	gm. fat	32.5	mg. calcium
28.0	gm. carbohydrate		

Chocolate Angel Cupcakes

If you have only twelve muffin pan cups, use two custard cups for the remaining batter.

1	cup sugar
1/2	cup all-purpose flour
1/4	cup unsweetened cocoa powder
6	large egg whites, at room temperature
1/2	teaspoon cream of tartar
1	teaspoon vanilla extract
1	tablespoon powdered sugar

Preheat oven to 375°. Place paper baking cups in fourteen muffin pan cups.

Sift sugar, flour and cocoa powder into a small bowl; set aside.

In a large mixer bowl at high speed, beat egg whites and cream of tartar until stiff but not dry. Sprinkle vanilla over egg whites. With a wire whisk or rubber scraper, fold in cocoa mixture, half at a time, until no white streaks remain. Spoon about 1/4 cup of the mixture into each paper baking cup.

Bake for 18 to 22 minutes or until tops spring back when touched. Remove cupcakes from muffin pans and cool on wire racks.

To serve, sprinkle with powdered sugar.

Makes 14 servings

Per serving:

86	calories
2.3	gm. protein
0.2	gm. fat
18.8	gm. carbohydrate
22.0	mg. sodium
0.0	mg. cholesterol
4.6	mg. calcium

Luscious Desserts

Lemon Soufflé

If desired, garnish soufflé with whipped cream and lemon slices.

2	envelopes unflavored gelatin
1	cup cold water
6	large egg yolks, beaten
1 1/2	cups sugar
1/4	teaspoon salt
4	large lemons
6	large egg whites, at room temperature
1 1/2	cups whipping cream, whipped

Measure around the outside of a 1 1/2-quart soufflé dish and add 3 inches. Cut a piece of foil that length and fold in half lengthwise. Butter the inside of the dish. Butter one side of the foil. Sprinkle dish with sugar and shake out excess. Wrap foil strip tightly around the dish so collar extends 2 to 3 inches above the rim. Fasten with tape; set aside.

In a small saucepan, mix gelatin and water; let stand for 1 minute. Stir in egg yolks, 1 cup of the sugar and salt. Stir over low heat for 5 minutes or until gelatin dissolves and mixture thickens slightly. Pour into a large bowl.

Grate lemon rind to make 2 tablespoons; set aside. Squeeze lemons to make 1 cup juice. Stir lemon rind and juice into gelatin mixture. Chill until mixture is the consistency of unbeaten egg whites.

In a small mixer bowl at high speed, beat egg whites until soft peaks form. Gradually beat in remaining 1/2 cup sugar and continue beating until stiff but not dry. Gently fold into gelatin mixture. Fold in whipped cream until no white streaks remain. Spoon into prepared dish. Chill at least 2 hours or until firm.

To serve, remove collar.

Makes 8 (about 1 cup) servings

Per serving:

374	calories	139.2	mg. sodium
7.3	gm. protein	268.5	mg. cholesterol
20.9	gm. fat	58.9	mg. calcium
41.7	gm. carbohydrate		

Luscious

Molded Strawberry Dessert

If you prefer, chill in individual molds or parfait glasses.

2	*packages (10 oz. each) frozen strawberries in heavy syrup, thawed*
2	*cups whipping cream*
3/4	*cup dairy sour cream*
4	*tablespoons sugar*
2	*envelopes unflavored gelatin*
1/2	*cup cold water*

Drain strawberries, reserving syrup. Set berries aside.

In a large bowl, mix 1 1/2 cups of the whipping cream, 1 1/4 cups of the reserved strawberry syrup, sour cream and 3 tablespoons of the sugar until sugar dissolves; set aside.

In a small saucepan, mix gelatin and water; let stand for 1 minute. Stir over low heat until gelatin dissolves. Stir into cream mixture until blended. Pour into a 4-cup mold. Chill for 1 hour or until set.

To serve, in a small mixer bowl at medium speed, beat remaining 1/2 cup whipping cream and remaining 1 tablespoon sugar until stiff peaks form.

Unmold chilled mixture onto a serving plate. Place strawberries in a blender container. Cover and blend at low speed for 30 seconds or until very smooth and shiny. Pour about 1/3 cup puréed strawberries over mold; top with whipped cream. Serve remaining berry sauce separately.

Makes 8 (about 1/2 cup) servings

Per serving:

332	calories
3.7	gm. protein
26.1	gm. fat
23.5	gm. carbohydrate
35.9	mg. sodium
91.5	mg. cholesterol
69.1	mg. calcium

Swedish Cream

Top with sweetened fresh fruit.

1	cup sugar
1	envelope unflavored gelatin
1	cup cold whipping cream
1	cup dairy sour cream
1/2	teaspoon vanilla extract

In a small saucepan, mix together sugar and gelatin. Stir in whipping cream; let stand for 1 minute. Stir over low heat for 5 minutes or until sugar dissolves. (Do not dissolve gelatin completely.)

In a medium bowl, stir sour cream and vanilla until smooth. Gradually stir in gelatin mixture until well blended. Pour into sherbet or parfait glasses and chill at least 1 hour or until set.

Makes 6 (about 1/2 cup) servings

Per serving:

341	calories
2.8	gm. protein
21.5	gm. fat
35.8	gm. carbohydrate
33.7	mg. sodium
69.3	mg. cholesterol
64.0	mg. calcium

Luscious

Brandy Alexander Cream

What a great choice for a special dinner party!

1	teaspoon unflavored gelatin
1/2	cup cold half-and-half
1/8	teaspoon salt
2	large eggs, separated
3/4	cup sugar
1/3	cup brandy
1/4	cup crème de cacao
1	cup whipping cream, whipped
1	cup whipping cream
2	tablespoons sugar
1/2	ounce coarsely grated semisweet chocolate (about 3 tablespoons)

In a small saucepan, mix gelatin and half-and-half; let stand for 1 minute. Add salt. Stir over low heat until gelatin dissolves.

Place egg yolks in a small bowl. Gradually stir gelatin mixture into egg yolks until blended, then return mixture to saucepan. Cook and stir over low heat until mixture coats a spoon (do not boil). Place saucepan in a bowl of cold water and ice. Stir egg mixture to cool quickly and stop the cooking. Stir in 1/2 cup of the sugar, brandy and crème de cacao. Stir gelatin mixture until slightly thickened. Remove saucepan from ice water.

In a small mixer bowl at high speed, beat egg whites until foamy. Gradually beat in 1/4 cup sugar and continue beating until stiff and glossy. Fold into gelatin mixture until no white streaks remain. Fold in whipped cream until blended. Spoon into ten individual stemmed glasses. Freeze at least 3 hours or overnight. About 15 minutes before serving, remove from freezer. In a small mixer bowl at medium speed, beat 1 cup whipping cream and 2 tablespoons sugar until stiff peaks form. Spoon onto desserts and sprinkle with chocolate.

Makes 10 (about 1/2 cup) servings

Per serving:

306	calories	64.0	mg. sodium
3.2	gm. protein	126.4	mg. cholesterol
20.7	gm. fat	52.1	mg. calcium
23.3	gm. carbohydrate		

Frosty Raspberry Squares

A good make-ahead for a summer buffet.

12	(2³/4-inch) crispy-style macaroon cookies
1	package (2 oz.) sliced almonds (¹/2 cup)
¹/4	cup margarine, cut in pieces
1	package (10 oz.) frozen red raspberries in heavy syrup, thawed
2/3	cup sugar
3	large egg whites, at room temperature
2	tablespoons lemon juice
1	container (4 oz.) frozen nondairy whipped topping, thawed

Preheat oven to 350°.

Break up macaroon cookies. Place in a food processor bowl or blender container. Cover and process or blend with on-off bursts to make coarse crumbs (you will need 1¹/2 cups).

In a 13 x 9 x 2-inch baking pan, place cookie crumbs and almonds. Dot with margarine. Bake for 12 to 15 minutes or until toasted and browned, stirring several times. Remove from oven and cool on a wire rack. Set ³/4 cup of the crumb mixture aside for topping. Spread remaining mixture evenly in pan.

In a large mixer bowl at low speed, beat raspberries with syrup, sugar, egg whites and lemon juice until foamy. Increase speed to medium-high and beat for 10 minutes or until stiff peaks form, scraping bowl occasionally. At low speed, beat in whipped topping until no white streaks remain. Spread evenly over cooled crumb mixture in baking pan. Smooth top. Sprinkle with reserved crumb mixture. Cover and freeze at least 8 hours or until firm. About 1 hour before serving, place covered pan in refrigerator. Cut into squares.

Makes 12 servings

Per serving:

256	calories
3.0	gm. protein
13.0	gm. fat
33.3	gm. carbohydrate
66.6	mg. sodium
0.0	mg. cholesterol
23.7	mg. calcium

Luscious

Cookies and Cream Log

Peanuts and chocolate—a popular combination!

2	*cups whipping cream*
1¹/2	*cups chopped chocolate peanut cluster candy (about 9 oz.)*
1	*box (9 oz.) chocolate wafer cookies*

In a small mixer bowl at medium speed, beat whipping cream until stiff peaks form. Fold in 1 cup of the candy.

Spread tops of each chocolate wafer with about 1 tablespoon of the whipped cream mixture. Make stacks of four or five cookies, then stand stacks on edge and make one long roll on a serving plate. Frost outside with remaining cream mixture. Sprinkle top with remaining candy. Chill at least 4 or up to 12 hours before serving.

To serve, slice diagonally.

Makes 12 servings

Per serving:

280	calories
4.6	gm. protein
24.3	gm. fat
13.1	gm. carbohydrate
28.7	mg. sodium
58.2	mg. cholesterol
53.5	mg. calcium

Cassata Riviera

A perfect ending for an Italian feast.

12	ounces ricotta cheese (about 1¹/₃ cups)
3	tablespoons sugar
2	cups whipping cream
¹/₄	cup orange liqueur or frozen orange juice concentrate, thawed
¹/₂	teaspoon grated orange rind
¹/₄	cup semisweet mini chocolate chips
3	tablespoons finely chopped candied orange peel
24	ladyfingers, split
3	tablespoons powdered sugar

In a small mixer bowl at low speed, beat ricotta cheese and sugar until smooth. Gradually beat in ¹/₂ cup of the whipping cream, orange liqueur or juice, and orange rind until blended. Stir in chocolate chips and candied orange peel; set aside.

Line bottom and sides of a 1¹/₂-quart bowl or mold with a layer of ladyfinger halves, trimming as needed. Spread one-third of the ricotta mixture over the bottom; cover with one-third of the remaining ladyfingers. Repeat twice. Press top gently to level surface. Cover with plastic wrap and chill at least 4 hours or overnight. To unmold, carefully run a metal spatula around inside of bowl. Unmold onto a serving plate.

In a small mixer bowl at medium speed, beat remaining 1¹/₂ cups whipping cream and powdered sugar until stiff peaks form. Frost and decorate cassata with whipped cream. Garnish with crystallized violets if desired. Refrigerate up to 4 hours. Cut with a sharp knife.

Makes 10 servings

Per serving (orange liqueur):		*Per serving (orange juice):*	
355	calories	345	calories
6.3	gm. protein	6.5	gm. protein
25.0	gm. fat	25.0	gm. fat
25.2	gm. carbohydrate	25.0	gm. carbohydrate
61.1	mg. sodium	61.0	mg. sodium
84.4	mg. cholesterol	84.4	mg. cholesterol
111.2	mg. calcium	113.3	mg. calcium

Rum Raisin Trifle

2/3   cup golden raisins

1/3   cup rum or orange juice

1   package (2 oz.) slivered almonds (about 1/2 cup)

1   package (3 oz.) vanilla cook & serve pudding and pie filling mix

2 1/2   cups half-and-half

1   cup whipping cream

1   package (10 3/4 oz.) frozen pound cake, thawed

4   tablespoons rum or orange juice

In a small bowl, combine raisins and 1/3 cup rum or orange juice. Let stand for 1 hour, stirring several times.

Preheat oven to 350°. In a shallow pan, toast almonds for 5 to 8 minutes, stirring occasionally; set aside.

In a medium saucepan, prepare pudding and pie filling mix according to package directions, substituting 2 1/2 cups half-and-half for milk. Cool to room temperature, stirring several times.

In a small mixer bowl at medium speed, beat 1/2 cup of the whipping cream until stiff peaks form. Fold into cooled pudding.

Cut cake into 3/4-inch cubes. Place about one-third of the cake in a 1 1/2-quart glass serving dish. Sprinkle with 2 tablespoons of the rum or orange juice. Layer one-third of the raisins, one-third of the pudding, one-third of the cake and sprinkle with 1 tablespoon of the rum or orange juice. Repeat layers ending with remaining pudding. Cover with plastic wrap and refrigerate 4 to 24 hours.

To serve, in a small mixer bowl at medium speed, beat remaining 1/2 cup whipping cream until stiff peaks form. Pipe or spoon on trifle. Serve immediately or refrigerate up to 1 hour. Just before serving, garnish with almonds.

Makes 8 servings

Per serving (with rum):		*Per serving (with orange juice):*	
519	calories	488	calories
7.5	gm. protein	7.6	gm. protein
30.8	gm. fat	30.8	gm. fat
46.1	gm. carbohydrate	48.2	gm. carbohydrate
160.2	mg. sodium	165.7	mg. sodium
132.5	mg. cholesterol	132.5	mg. cholesterol
141.4	mg. calcium	141.6	mg. calcium

Bananas Caramel

Can be served over ice cream if desired.

1/4	cup packed brown sugar
1/4	cup sugar
1	tablespoon all-purpose flour
1/2	cup whipping cream
2	tablespoons banana-flavored liqueur
3	tablespoons butter
1	teaspoon vanilla extract
1/4	teaspoon ground nutmeg
4	medium, firm, ripe bananas, peeled
1/4	cup coarsely chopped pecans

In a 1-quart saucepan, mix brown sugar, sugar and flour. Stir in cream until smooth. Stirring over medium heat, bring to a boil and boil for 3 minutes or until thick and glossy. Remove from heat.

Stir in liqueur, 1 tablespoon of the butter, vanilla and nutmeg; set aside.

Halve bananas crosswise, then lengthwise. In a 10-inch skillet over medium heat, melt remaining 2 tablespoons butter. Add bananas, turning to coat with butter. Place cut-side down and cook until lightly browned. Stir sauce into butter and baste bananas until coated.

Spoon bananas and sauce into a serving dish and sprinkle with nuts.

Makes 4 servings

Per serving:

466	calories
2.6	gm. protein
24.9	gm. fat
59.4	gm. carbohydrate
105.4	mg. sodium
65.2	mg. cholesterol
44.4	mg. calcium

Spiced Cranberries Jubilee

Flaming a dessert is fun and impressive.

1   cup fresh cranberries, washed

2/3   cup orange marmalade

1/2   cup sugar

1   teaspoon ground cinnamon

1/3   cup brandy or orange liqueur

3   cups vanilla ice cream

In a 1-quart saucepan over medium heat, combine cranberries, marmalade, sugar and cinnamon. Bring to a boil, reduce heat to low and simmer for 8 to 10 minutes or until cranberries burst and mixture is syrupy, stirring occasionally. Can be made up to 2 hours before serving. If making ahead, cover and set aside.

If necessary, reheat cranberry mixture. Transfer to a warm chafing dish. In a small saucepan, warm brandy or liqueur. Immediately pour over cranberries and ignite. Stir to blend until flame dies.

Serve hot mixture over ice cream.

Makes 6 servings

Per serving (brandy):		*Per serving (orange liqueur):*	
365	calories	389	calories
2.5	gm. protein	2.5	gm. protein
12.0	gm. fat	12.0	gm. fat
60.9	gm. carbohydrate	64.6	gm. carbohydrate
62.4	mg. sodium	62.0	mg. sodium
44.0	mg. cholesterol	44.0	mg. cholesterol
89.5	mg. calcium	88.4	mg. calcium

Bread Pudding

This is a traditional Southern dessert. Serve with Bourbon Sauce.

1/4	cup margarine, cut in pieces
	Day-old French bread (about 8 oz.)
1/4	cup raisins
2 1/2	cups half-and-half
1	cup sugar
1	teaspoon ground cinnamon
3	large eggs
2	large egg yolks
3	teaspoons vanilla extract
1/8	teaspoon salt
2	tablespoons powdered sugar

Place top oven shelf 8 inches from heat source. Preheat oven to 350°. Place margarine in a shallow 1 1/2-quart baking dish and melt in oven.

Trim crusts from bread and tear into small pieces (you will need 6 cups). Place in melted margarine and toss until coated. Evenly spread in dish. Sprinkle with raisins; set aside.

In a saucepan over medium heat, heat half-and-half to just under boiling (do not boil). Remove from heat.

In a small bowl, mix sugar and cinnamon; set aside.

In a medium bowl, beat eggs and egg yolks. Stir in sugar-cinnamon, vanilla and salt until well blended. Slowly stir in hot half-and-half. Evenly pour over bread and raisins. Bake on top shelf of oven for 45 minutes or until a knife inserted in center comes out clean.

Sprinkle top of bread pudding with powdered sugar. Turn oven temperature to broil. Broil for 1 minute or until lightly browned. Top will collapse while cooling. Serve warm.

Makes 8 servings

Per serving:

404	calories		322.2	mg. sodium
8.0	gm. protein		200.7	mg. cholesterol
18.7	gm. fat		117.8	mg. calcium
50.9	gm. carbohydrate			

Luscious

Bourbon Sauce

The alcohol evaporates during cooking, leaving only the flavor.

2/3	cup packed brown sugar
1	tablespoon cornstarch
1	cup milk
2	large egg yolks, well beaten
1/4	cup margarine
1/4	cup bourbon whiskey
1	teaspoon vanilla extract

In a small saucepan, mix brown sugar and cornstarch. Stir in milk until smooth. Stirring over medium heat, bring to a boil and boil for 1 minute or until thick and glossy.

Gradually stir into egg yolks until blended, then return mixture to saucepan. Cook and stir over low heat for 1 minute (do not boil). Remove from heat.

Stir in margarine until melted. Stir in bourbon and vanilla until blended. Serve warm over Bread Pudding, sliced pound cake, baked apples or baked bananas.

If making ahead, place a piece of plastic wrap or waxed paper directly on surface of sauce and refrigerate. Reheat over low heat before serving.

Makes about 2 1/4 cups

Per 1/4-cup serving:

157	calories
1.6	gm. protein
7.2	gm. fat
17.8	gm. carbohydrate
79.4	mg. sodium
64.1	mg. cholesterol
53.7	mg. calcium

Lemon Puffs

For variety, fill cream puffs with ice cream.

3/4   cup water

5   tablespoons butter

1/4   teaspoon salt

3/4   cup all-purpose flour

3   large eggs

1   large egg, beaten
    Creamy Lemon Filling (see page 47)

1   cup strawberry topping for ice cream

Preheat oven to 375°. Lightly grease a baking sheet.

In a medium saucepan, combine water, butter and salt. Over high heat, bring to a boil. When butter melts, stir in flour all at once and stir vigorously until mixture forms a ball. Remove from heat.

Beat in 3 eggs, one at a time, until smooth and shiny. Drop mixture onto baking sheet, forming eight mounds, using about 1/4 cup of dough for each. Flatten tops slightly. Brush with beaten egg.

Bake for 30 to 40 minutes or until puffed and golden brown. Cut top off each cream puff. Cool completely on a wire rack.

To serve, remove moist inside dough. Fill each puff with 1/4 cup Creamy Lemon Filling. Replace top. Arrange puffs in a circle on a large serving platter. Spoon on strawberry topping.

Makes 8

Per serving:

385   calories
7.9   gm. protein
14.3   gm. fat
57.8   gm. carbohydrate
237.9   mg. sodium
266.6   mg. cholesterol
115.2   mg. calcium

Creamy Lemon Filling

Use this lemony, but not too tart, filling for Lemon Puffs.

3/4	cup sugar
1/3	cup all-purpose flour
	Dash salt
2	cups milk
3	large egg yolks, lightly beaten
2	large lemons

In a medium saucepan, mix sugar, flour and salt. Stir in milk. Stirring over medium heat, bring to a boil and boil for 8 to 10 minutes or until very thick and glossy.

Gradually stir about one-third of the hot mixture into egg yolks, then stir back into hot mixture in saucepan. Cook and stir over low heat 2 minutes longer (do not boil). Remove from heat.

Grate lemon rind to make 1 tablespoon; set aside. Squeeze lemons to make 1/2 cup juice. Stir lemon rind and juice into cooked mixture. Chill at least 1 hour. Stir before using as a filling for Lemon Puffs.

Makes a generous 2 cups

Per 1/4-cup serving:

155	calories
3.7	gm. protein
4.2	gm. fat
26.5	gm. carbohydrate
49.5	mg. sodium
110.2	mg. cholesterol
87.1	mg. calcium

Sweetheart Torte

If using a blender to grind the almonds, do it in two batches.

3	packages (2 oz. each) blanched almonds (about 1 1/2 cups total)
1 1/4	cups sugar
6	large egg whites, at room temperature
1/8	teaspoon salt
3	tablespoons sugar
1 1/2	teaspoons vanilla extract
6	ounces semisweet chocolate, chopped
2 1/2	cups whipping cream
1/4	cup butter
1/4	cup powdered sugar

Preheat oven to 250°. Grease and flour three baking sheets. With the tip of a knife, draw an 8-inch circle or heart on each baking sheet.

Place almonds and 1 cup of the sugar in a food processor bowl. Cover and process until nuts are finely ground; set aside.

In a large mixer bowl at high speed, beat egg whites and salt until soft peaks form. Gradually beat in 3 tablespoons sugar and vanilla and continue beating until stiff peaks form. Gently fold in sugared ground almonds. Spread one-third of the mixture in each circle on baking sheets.

Bake for 50 to 55 minutes or until nearly dry and edges are golden. Loosen layers with a spatula and carefully transfer shells to wire racks to cool. Assemble torte immediately or store meringues in an airtight container.

In a small saucepan, mix chocolate, 1/2 cup of the whipping cream, remaining 1/4 cup sugar and butter. Stirring constantly over low heat, cook until chocolate melts and mixture is smooth. Chill for 1 hour or until firm enough to spread.

In a small mixer bowl at medium speed, beat remaining 2 cups whipping cream and powdered sugar until stiff peaks form.

About 4 1/2 hours before serving, assemble torte. Place one meringue layer on a serving plate and spread with about 1 cup of the whipped cream. Spread half of the chocolate mixture on a second meringue layer; place chocolate-side down on first layer. Spread about 1 cup of

Luscious

the whipped cream on the top surface. Spread remaining chocolate mixture on third meringue layer; place chocolate-side down on cream-covered stack. Wrap assembled torte in plastic wrap and chill for 3 1/2 hours.

Uncover and frost top and sides of torte with remaining whipped cream. Chill, uncovered, for 30 minutes before serving.

Makes 16 servings

Per serving:

356	calories
4.6	gm. protein
26.1	gm. fat
29.3	gm. carbohydrate
80.7	mg. sodium
60.2	mg. cholesterol
59.1	mg. calcium

Frozen Fudge Fantasy

Wonderful plain, but fabulous with Raspberry Sauce.

	Unsweetened cocoa powder
3	cups (18 oz.) semisweet chocolate chips
1	pound butter, cut in small pieces
2¹/4	cups sugar
1	cup boiling water
9	large eggs
1	cup whipping cream, whipped

Preheat oven to 250°. Lightly coat the bottom and sides of a 9 x 3-inch springform pan with butter. Dust with unsweetened cocoa powder.

In a large saucepan, mix chocolate chips, butter, sugar and boiling water. Over medium-low heat, cook until melted and smooth, stirring occasionally. Remove from heat.

Whisk in eggs, one at a time, until blended. Pour into springform pan. Place on a baking sheet.

Bake for 2 hours. Turn oven off. With oven door open, let cool in oven for 30 minutes. Cool completely on a wire rack (it may flatten and possibly crack on top).

Release and remove side of springform pan. Place dessert top-side down on a piece of plastic wrap. Remove metal bottom. Cover with plastic wrap, then foil, and freeze at least 12 hours.

To serve, pipe top with whipped cream and garnish with chocolate curls, raspberries and mint leaves if desired. Serve frozen. Slice in thin wedges.

Makes 20 servings

Per serving:

456	calories
4.2	gm. protein
34.4	gm. fat
37.6	gm. carbohydrate
224.4	mg. sodium
189.7	mg. cholesterol
34.1	mg. calcium

Luscious

Raspberry Sauce

Adds a light touch to a rich dessert.

    1   *package (10 oz.) frozen red raspberries in heavy syrup, thawed*
  1/4   *cup orange liqueur*

Place raspberries and syrup in a blender container. Cover and blend until puréed. Press mixture through a sieve with a rubber scraper to remove seeds. Stir in liqueur.

Serve over Frozen Fudge Fantasy, ice cream, slices of angel food cake or dessert of your choice.

Makes 1 1/4 cups

Per 1-tablespoon serving:

   24   calories
  0.1   gm. protein
  0.0   gm. fat
  4.9   gm. carbohydrate
  0.2   mg. sodium
  0.0   mg. cholesterol
  2.2   mg. calcium

$\mathscr{B}$aklava

Truly special but not difficult to make.

1	*pound walnuts, finely chopped*
1½	*cups sugar*
2	*teaspoons ground cinnamon*
1	*package (16 oz.) frozen phyllo pastry leaves, thawed*
1¾	*cups butter, melted*
1	*cup water*
2	*tablespoons lemon juice*
1	*cup honey*
½	*teaspoon vanilla extract*

Preheat oven to 300°. Lightly butter the bottom of a 15½ x 10½ x 1-inch jelly roll pan.

In a medium bowl, combine walnuts, ½ cup of the sugar and cinnamon; set aside.

Unfold pastry leaves and cover with a damp towel to prevent drying out. Carefully fit one whole pastry leaf into jelly roll pan (edges will extend over the sides); lightly brush with butter. Repeat until six leaves have been stacked. Spread with 1 cup of the walnut mixture.

Cut remaining pastry leaves in half crosswise. Layer eight half leaves, staggering each to fit inside the pan and lightly brushing each with butter. Spread with 1 cup walnut mixture. Repeat twice.

Layer the remaining half leaves on top, lightly brushing each with butter. Brush top with remaining butter. Trim edges if necessary. With a sharp knife, cut halfway through layers, making five lengthwise cuts to form six equal strips. Cut diagonally to make about forty-eight pieces.

Bake for 1 hour or until golden brown. Finish cutting through layers to bottom.

Meanwhile, in a medium saucepan, combine remaining 1 cup sugar, water and lemon juice. Stirring occasionally over medium-high heat, cook for 12 to 15 minutes or until syrupy; remove from heat.

Stir in honey and vanilla until well blended. Pour over hot Baklava. Cool to room temperature. Cover lightly and let stand at room temperature at least 24 hours to mellow. Store tightly covered in a cool place.

Note: *The top layers of the Baklava need to be scored before baking because they become very crisp and brittle when baked. To obtain the traditional diamond-shaped pieces, first cut lengthwise, then on the diagonal as shown. The pieces at the short ends will be triangles instead of diamonds.*

Makes about 48 servings

Per serving:

196	calories
2.5	gm. protein
12.6	gm. fat
20.2	gm. carbohydrate
69.6	mg. sodium
18.1	mg. cholesterol
12.4	mg. calcium

Raspberry Crowns

If patty shells are baked ahead, re-crisp in a 350° oven.

1	package (10 oz.) frozen patty shells
1	package (12 oz.) frozen dry pack red raspberries
1/4	cup margarine
1	package (2 oz.) sliced almonds (about 1/2 cup)
2	tablespoons brown sugar
2	cups whipping cream
1/4	cup sugar
2	teaspoons vanilla extract
1/2	cup orange marmalade
2	tablespoons sugar

Bake patty shells according to package directions. Remove center of top and soft pastry underneath. Cool on a wire rack.

Place unopened package of raspberries in a large bowl of hot tap water until berries are no longer icy.

In an 8-inch nonstick skillet over medium heat, melt margarine. Add almonds and brown sugar. Stir for 4 minutes or until almonds are golden and foam subsides. Spread in a jelly roll pan to cool. Break apart and set aside.

In a small mixer bowl at medium speed, beat whipping cream, 1/4 cup sugar and vanilla until very stiff. Refrigerate until ready to assemble.

In a small saucepan over low heat, melt marmalade. Cool slightly.

Remove raspberries from bag and drain; sprinkle with 2 tablespoons sugar. Place each patty shell on an individual dessert plate. Spoon whipped cream into a large decorating bag fitted with a large star tube. Pipe a small mound of cream in center of each patty shell. Top with one-sixth of the raspberries. Drizzle about 1 tablespoon of the marmalade around berries. Pipe cream swirls around base of shell. Sprinkle almonds around swirls. Repeat to make remaining desserts.

Makes 6 servings

Per serving:

794	calories	308.9	mg. sodium
6.8	gm. protein	112.0	mg. cholesterol
59.8	gm. fat	110.0	mg. calcium
62.0	gm. carbohydrate		

Luscious

Rich Cheesecake

Top with berries or canned cherry pie filling.

1¹/2   cups graham cracker crumbs
¹/2   cup finely chopped walnuts
¹/2   cup margarine, melted
¹/4   cup sugar
5   packages (8 oz. each) cream cheese, softened
1²/3   cups sugar
6   large eggs
1   cup dairy sour cream
3   tablespoons all-purpose flour
1   tablespoon grated lemon or orange rind
2   teaspoons vanilla extract
¹/4   teaspoon salt

In a medium bowl, mix graham cracker crumbs, walnuts, margarine and ¹/4 cup sugar. Press mixture evenly against bottom and 2 inches up sides of a 10 x 3-inch springform pan. Chill for 30 minutes.

Preheat oven to 475°. In a large mixer bowl at medium speed, beat cream cheese until smooth. At low speed, slowly add 1²/3 cups sugar, beating until smooth. Add eggs, sour cream, flour, grated rind, vanilla and salt; beat for 3 minutes or until smooth. Carefully pour mixture into crust.

Bake for 15 minutes. Reduce heat to 200° and bake 1 hour and 15 minutes longer. Turn oven off and leave cake in closed oven for 30 minutes. Cool on a wire rack for 30 minutes. Cover and chill at least 8 hours or until ready to serve.

Makes 20 servings

Per serving:

409	calories
7.4	gm. protein
30.5	gm. fat
27.7	gm. carbohydrate
303.8	mg. sodium
148.2	mg. cholesterol
73.2	mg. calcium

Peanut Butter Mousse Pie

Chill the pie overnight to allow flavors to blend.

1/3	cup semisweet chocolate chips
2	teaspoons vegetable oil
1	envelope unflavored gelatin
3/4	cup cold water
1	package (8 oz.) cream cheese, softened
1	cup sugar
1	cup dairy sour cream
2/3	cup creamy peanut butter
2	teaspoons vanilla extract
1	cup frozen nondairy whipped topping, thawed
1	ready-made chocolate crumb pie crust

In a small saucepan over low heat, cook chocolate chips and oil until chocolate melts (do not burn). Remove from heat; set aside.

In another small saucepan, mix gelatin and water; let stand for 1 minute. Stir over low heat until gelatin dissolves. Remove from heat; set aside.

In a large mixer bowl at medium-high speed, beat cream cheese, sugar, sour cream, peanut butter and vanilla until fluffy. Gradually beat in gelatin mixture. Place bowl of peanut butter mixture in a larger bowl of cold water and ice. Stir peanut butter mixture until it mounds when dropped from a spoon.

Fold in whipped topping. Mound into pie crust, making a swirl in the center. Drizzle with chocolate mixture. Chill to set.

Makes 8 servings

Per serving:

598	calories
11.7	gm. protein
42.0	gm. fat
48.4	gm. carbohydrate
199.7	mg. sodium
41.0	mg. cholesterol
76.3	mg. calcium

Luscious

Cocoa Pecan Pie

An old favorite with a new twist.

1	cup sugar
1/3	cup unsweetened cocoa powder
1/4	cup all-purpose flour
1/2	teaspoon salt
3/4	cup dark corn syrup
3/4	cup half-and-half
3	large eggs, lightly beaten
1/4	cup margarine, melted
1	teaspoon vanilla extract
1	cup pecan halves
1	unbaked 9-inch pie shell

Preheat oven to 325°. In a small bowl, mix sugar, cocoa powder, flour and salt; set aside.

In a large bowl, mix corn syrup, half-and-half, eggs, margarine and vanilla. Stir in dry ingredients until smooth. Stir in pecans. Pour into pie shell.

Bake for 60 to 70 minutes or until a knife inserted halfway between center and edge comes out clean. Cool completely on a wire rack.

Serve at room temperature. Refrigerate leftovers.

Makes 8 servings

Per serving:

529	calories
6.7	gm. protein
27.5	gm. fat
65.3	gm. carbohydrate
438.4	mg. sodium
111.7	mg. cholesterol
51.2	mg. calcium

French Silk Pie

A chocolate lover's dream come true.

2	*cups shredded coconut*
1/4	*cup margarine, melted*
1	*cup margarine, softened*
1	*cup sugar*
2	*large eggs*
1/2	*cup chopped walnuts*
2	*ounces unsweetened chocolate, melted*
2	*tablespoons instant coffee powder*
1 1/2	*tablespoons brandy or rum*
1/3	*cup chopped walnuts*

Preheat oven to 375°.

In a small bowl, mix coconut and melted margarine until coconut is well coated. Press mixture against bottom and sides of a 9-inch pie plate.

Bake for 8 to 10 minutes or until edges are golden. Cool on a wire rack. Chill while preparing filling.

In a small mixer bowl at medium speed, beat softened margarine and sugar until fluffy. Add eggs, one at a time, beating for 3 minutes after each addition.

Stir in 1/2 cup walnuts, chocolate, coffee powder and brandy or rum. Spoon into coconut crust and chill at least 2 hours.

To serve, sprinkle with 1/3 cup walnuts.

Makes 8 servings

Per serving:

604	calories
5.3	gm. protein
48.5	gm. fat
41.0	gm. carbohydrate
415.1	mg. sodium
68.5	mg. cholesterol
40.3	mg. calcium

Mocha Cream Cake

A great do-ahead. Impressive looking, too.

1	cup butter, softened
2	cups powdered sugar
1/2	cup unsweetened cocoa powder
1/4	cup hot water
2	teaspoons instant coffee powder
1	teaspoon ground cinnamon
1	loaf (16 oz.) pound cake, thawed if frozen
1/3	cup coffee liqueur

In a large mixer bowl at high speed, beat butter until creamy. At low speed, gradually add powdered sugar, beating until fluffy.

In a small bowl, blend cocoa powder, water, coffee powder and cinnamon; add by teaspoonfuls to butter mixture, beating until well blended. Reserve 1/2 cup frosting.

Cut cake into three layers. Place bottom layer on a serving plate. Brush with one-third of the liqueur. Frost the top with 1/2 cup of the frosting; repeat stacking layers of cake, brushing with liqueur and frosting with buttercream. Frost top and sides of cake. Pipe with reserved 1/2 cup frosting. Cover loosely and chill at least 3 hours or overnight.

About 1 hour before serving, remove cake from refrigerator.

Makes 12 servings

Per serving:

412	calories
3.5	gm. protein
25.1	gm. fat
41.5	gm. carbohydrate
285.6	mg. sodium
86.6	mg. cholesterol
30.3	mg. calcium

Portland Hazelnut Torte

Hazelnuts, pecans, almonds or walnuts can be used.

2	cups hazelnuts (about 8 oz.)
8	large egg yolks
1	cup sugar
1/3	cup fine dry bread crumbs
1 1/4	teaspoons baking powder
1	teaspoon vanilla extract
1/8	teaspoon salt
10	large egg whites, at room temperature
2	tablespoons powdered sugar
	Chocolate Buttercream (see page 62)
1/4	cup chopped hazelnuts

Preheat oven to 325°. Grease a 15 1/2 x 10 1/2 x 1-inch jelly roll pan. Line with a piece of waxed paper long enough to extend about 1 inch over ends of pan; grease well and set aside.

Place 2 cups nuts in a food processor bowl or in a blender container. Cover and process or blend with on-off bursts until nuts are finely ground, scraping sides of bowl as needed. Do not grind too finely.

In a small mixer bowl at medium speed, beat egg yolks until thick and pale yellow. Add sugar and beat until very thick. Add ground nuts, bread crumbs, baking powder, vanilla and salt; beat until well blended. Transfer to a large bowl. Wash beaters.

In a large mixer bowl at high speed, beat egg whites until stiff peaks form. Stir about 1 cup of the whites into nut mixture to lighten. Fold in remaining egg whites just until blended. Spread batter evenly in pan.

Bake for 35 minutes or until lightly browned and edges pull away from pan. Lightly sprinkle top of hot cake with powdered sugar. Invert cake onto a large clean dish towel; peel off waxed paper. Cool.

To assemble, cut cake crosswise into four equal strips, each 10^1/$_2$ x 3^1/$_2$ inches. Place one cake strip on a serving plate. Frost the top with 2 tablespoons of the buttercream; repeat stacking layers of cake and frosting with buttercream.

Frost top and sides of cake. Pipe on a decorative design with buttercream. Garnish with chopped hazelnuts. Cover loosely and chill at least 3 hours or overnight.

About 1 hour before serving, remove from refrigerator. To serve, cut 1-inch slices with serrated knife.

Makes 10 servings

Per serving:

608	calories
10.9	gm. protein
40.7	gm. fat
53.6	gm. carbohydrate
327.6	mg. sodium
321.6	mg. cholesterol
115.8	mg. calcium

Chocolate Buttercream

Makes any ordinary cake extraordinary.

1	cup butter, softened
2	cups powdered sugar
1/3	cup unsweetened cocoa powder
1/4	cup hot water
1/2	teaspoon vanilla extract

In a small mixer bowl at medium speed, beat butter until creamy and fluffy.

Onto a sheet of waxed paper, sift powdered sugar and cocoa powder. At low speed, gradually add sugar mixture to butter and continue beating until smooth and fluffy.

Add hot water and vanilla; beat until well blended and of spreading consistency. Use for Portland Hazelnut Torte (see page 60) or on cake of your choice.

Makes about 2 1/3 cups

Per 1 tablespoon:

74	calories
0.4	gm. protein
5.2	gm. fat
6.6	gm. carbohydrate
49.9	mg. sodium
27.4	mg. cholesterol
3.9	mg. calcium

Banana Walnut Cake

1¹/4	cups chopped walnuts
2	cups all-purpose flour
¹/2	teaspoon salt
¹/2	teaspoon baking soda
¹/2	teaspoon baking powder
1¹/4	cups sugar
¹/2	cup margarine, softened
2	large eggs
¹/2	cup buttermilk
1	cup mashed ripe bananas (about 3 small)
¹/4	cup raspberry preserves, strained
1	small banana, sliced
	Cream Cheese Frosting (see page 64)
10	walnut halves

Preheat oven to 350°. Grease two 8 x 1-inch round cake pans. Line with waxed paper; grease and flour the paper.

In a shallow pan, toast chopped walnuts for 5 to 8 minutes.

Into a medium bowl, sift flour, salt, baking soda and baking powder.

In a large mixer bowl at medium speed, beat sugar and margarine until creamy. Beat in eggs. At low speed, beat in flour mixture in three additions alternately with buttermilk. Increase speed to medium and beat for 3 minutes. At low speed, beat in mashed bananas and 1/2 cup of the toasted walnuts just until blended. Pour into pans. Bake for 30 minutes or until a wooden pick inserted in center comes out clean. Cool in pans on wire racks for 10 minutes. Remove from pans, peel off waxed paper and cool layers completely on wire racks.

Place one layer on a cake plate. Spread with preserves. Top with banana slices. Cover with second cake layer. Frost top and sides. Pat remaining 3/4 cup toasted nuts on side of cake. Arrange walnut halves on top. Refrigerate leftovers.

Makes 10 servings

Per serving:

681	calories	374.6	mg. sodium
8.5	gm. protein	73.8	mg. cholesterol
30.1	gm. fat	72.9	mg. calcium
99.2	gm. carbohydrate		

Luscious

Cream Cheese Frosting

If frosting is too soft, refrigerate before serving.

2   *packages (3 oz. each) cream cheese, softened*
2   *tablespoons margarine, softened*
1   *teaspoon vanilla extract*
3   *cups powdered sugar*

In a small mixer bowl at low speed, beat cream cheese, margarine and vanilla until smooth. Gradually beat in powdered sugar, scraping bowl as needed. Increase speed to medium and beat until fluffy and of spreading consistency. Use on Banana Walnut Cake or on cake of your choice. Refrigerate leftovers.

Makes about 1 3/4 cups

Per 1 tablespoon:

79	calories
0.5	gm. protein
2.9	gm. fat
13.0	gm. carbohydrate
27.7	mg. sodium
6.6	mg. cholesterol
5.2	mg. calcium